Lindsay Sloper

Hanover Square

A Magazine of Pianoforte and Vocal Music

Lindsay Sloper

Hanover Square
A Magazine of Pianoforte and Vocal Music

ISBN/EAN: 9783744793179

Printed in Europe, USA, Canada, Australia, Japan

Cover: Foto ©Thomas Meinert / pixelio.de

More available books at **www.hansebooks.com**

MAY, 1869

HANOVER SQUARE,

A Magazine

OF

PIANOFORTE AND VOCAL MUSIC,

Edited by

LINDSAY SLOPER.

London.

CASSELL, PETTER & GALPIN.

"HANOVER SQUARE,"
A Magazine of New Copyright Music,
EDITED BY LINDSAY SLOPER.

VOLS. I. II. AND III. NOW READY.
Price, elegantly bound in cloth, SEVEN SHILLINGS AND SIXPENCE EACH.

CONTENTS OF VOL. I.

No. 1.
Sorrows and Joys. Sketch for the Pianoforte ... Jules Benedict.
What does Little Birdie say? Song ... Arthur S. Sullivan.
Bright Hours. Caprice. Piano ... Sydney Smith.
Bessie Bell. Ballad ... Henry Smart.

No. 2.
Notturno. Pianoforte ... E. Silas.
Change upon Change. Song ... Virginia Gabriel.
  The Words by Elizabeth Barrett Browning.
The Gipsies' Revel. Piece for the Pianoforte ... Wilhelm Kuhe.
Though Age be like December. Song ... M. W. Balfe.
  The Words by Campbell Clarke.

No. 3.
Felice Notte. Barcarolle for the Pianoforte ... Ernst Pauer.
A Voice from the Sea. Song ... J. L. Hatton.
  The Words by W. S. Passmore.
Twelfth Night. Valse de Salon ... Brinley Richards.
The King's Daughter. Song ... Alex. Reichardt.
  The Words by Heinrich Heine. Translated by Wellington Guernsey.

No. 4.
By the Lake. Reverie ... Lindsay Sloper.
Savourneen Deelish. Song ... Angelina.
  The Words by George Colman the younger.
Snowdrops. Pianoforte Piece ... Boyton Smith.
Forget Me Not. Song ... Wilhelm Ganz.
  The Words by Miss L. B. Courtenay.

No. 5.
Reveries-Valses. Piano ... Stephen Heller.
Kissing Her Hair. Song ... James L. Molloy.
  The Words by Algernon Charles Swinburne.
Galop de Concert. Piano ... Walter Macfarren.
River, Oh! River. Song ... Elizabeth Philp.

No. 6.
Impromptu. Piano ... Lefébure Wely.
Echoes. Song ... Virginia Gabriel.
  The Words by Christina Rosetti.
Serenade. Piano ... Henry W. Goodban.
Stall' ne Allegro. Stornello ... Alberto Randegger.
  The English Translation by Campbell Clarke.

CONTENTS OF VOL. II.

No. 7.
Evening Rest. Berceuse. Piano ... Sydney Smith.
Love, the Pilgrim. Song ... Jacques Blumenthal.
  The Words by Hamilton Aidé.
Spring Breezes. Pianoforte Piece ... Ignace Gibsone.
It is the Golden May-time. Song ... J. L. Hatton.
  The Words by B. S. Montgomery.

No. 8.
A Lullaby. Pianoforte Piece ... Charles Salaman.
O fair Dove! O fond Dove! Song ... Arthur S. Sullivan.
  The Words by Miss Jean Ingelow.
La Vivandière. Marche brillante. Piano ... Edouard de Paris.
Sunshine after Cloud. Song ... Clara Gottschalk.
  The Words by W. Harrison.

No. 9.
A Moonlight Walk. Pianoforte ... G. A. Osborne.
Sleep, my Baby, Mother's near. A Slumber Song Albert Leaf.
Hunting Song. Impromptu for Piano ... C. Swinnerton Heap (Mendelssohn Scholar).
Nobody's nigh to hear ... G. A. Macfarren.
  The Words by Miss Jean Ingelow.

No. 10.
Murmures. Nocturne-étude. Piano ... Charles A. Palmer
It was a Lover and his Lass. Song ... F. Stanislaus.
  The Words by Shakespeare.
L'Etincelle. Morceau de Salon. Piano ... René Favarger.
Little Blossom. Ballad ... Virginia Gabriel.
  The Words by Alfred Thompson.

No. 11.
Flower-de-Luce. Reverie. Piano ... Walter Macfarren.
The Butterfly and the Flower. Song ... Alberto Randegger
Le Sourire. Mazurka de Salon. Piano ... Henri Roubier.
Twenty Years Ago. Ballad ... E. L. Hime.
  The Words by J. E. Carpenter.

No. 12.
Shadow and Sunlight. Piano Piece ... W. Kuhe.
Ah, Love! Ballad ... F. Hawtree.
  The Words by Longfellow.
Felice. Valse de Salon. Piano ... Lindsay Sloper.
Two Summer Days. Song ... Michael Watson.

CONTENTS OF VOL. III.

No. 13.
Happy Memories. Morceau de Salon. Piano Sydney Smith.
A Farewell. Song ... Virginia Gabriel.
  The Words by Mrs. Frances Anne Kemble.
Bergeronnette, Styrienne. Piano ... M. Bergson.
Nora Creina. Song ... Alexander S. Cooper.
  The Words by Thomas Moore

No. 14.
Cantabile. Piano ... Charles Wehle.
Mary. Song ... G. A. Macfarren.
  The Words by Sir Walter Scott.
Rêve Espagnol. Serenade. Piano ... Edwin M. Lott.
'Twas long, long since, in the Spring time. Song G. B. Allen.
  The Words by Tom Hood.

No. 15.
Marche de Concert. Piano ... Walter Macfarren.
Wayward Thoughts. Song ... T. M. Mudie.
  The Words by Mrs. R. H. Foster.
Tears of Joy. Capriccietto ... Francesco Berger.
Ah! Chloris. Pastoral ... Ignace Gibsone.
  The Words by Sir Charles Sedley.

No. 16.
Idylle. Piano ... C. Neustedt.
Oh! to be a Sportive Fairy. Song ... J. L. Hatton.
  The Words by B. S. Montgomery.
The Song of the Brook. Pianoforte Piece ... E. A. Sydenham.
When Twilight Dews are falling soft. Song ... Evelyn Hampton.
  The Words by Thomas Moore.

No. 17.
Patrouille. Ronde de Nuit. Piano ... D. Magnus
Spinning Song ... Virginia Gabriel.
  The Words by W. Storey.
Dancing Sea Spray. Morceau de Salon. Piano J. Theodore Trekell.
Autumn Song ... Henry Smart.
  The Words from the German.

No. 18.
Serenade. Piano ... Frederick H. Cowen
Why, Lovely Charmer? Song ... E. A. Sydenham.
  The Words by Sir Richard Steele.
L'Inconstante. Valse de Salon. Piano Polydore de Vos
By the Sea. Ballad ... G. Richardson.
  The Words by C. O'Neill.

The separate Numbers are still to be had, Price ONE SHILLING EACH

The EXTRA CHRISTMAS NUMBER consists entirely of New Dance Music. Price One Shilling.
Kellogg-Valse, Arditi.—Marie (Polka Mazurka), Gung'l.—L'Ancien Regime (Quadrille on Old French Airs), Henry W. Goodban.
Blush-Rose Waltz, Charles Godfrey.—Tintamarre Galop, Charles de Manéren

LONDON. ASHDOWN AND PARRY, HANOVER SQUARE.

SUNRISE.

BY

J. F. BARNETT.

ZEPHYR, SHOULD'ST THOU CHANCE.

SONG

Composed by

The Rev? Sir **F. A. G. OUSELEY.** B?

Mus: Doc: & **M. A.**

JEÛNESSE DORÉE

GALOP DE CONCERT
PAR
SYDNEY SMITH.
Op: 88.

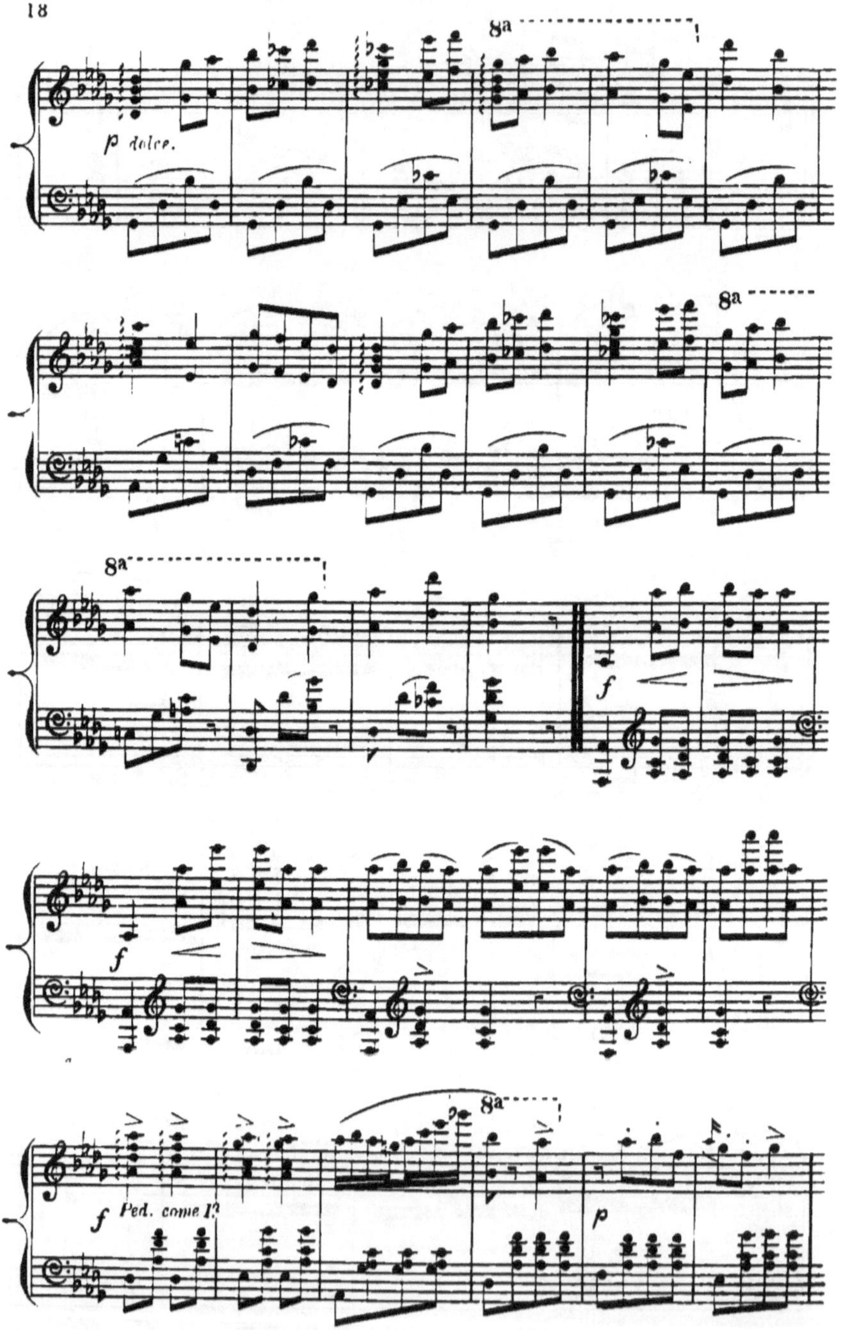
8a
p dolce.
8a
8a
f
f
f Ped. come I?
8a
p

O MISTRESS MINE.

SONG

Words by
SHAKSPEARE.

Music by
F. STANISLAUS

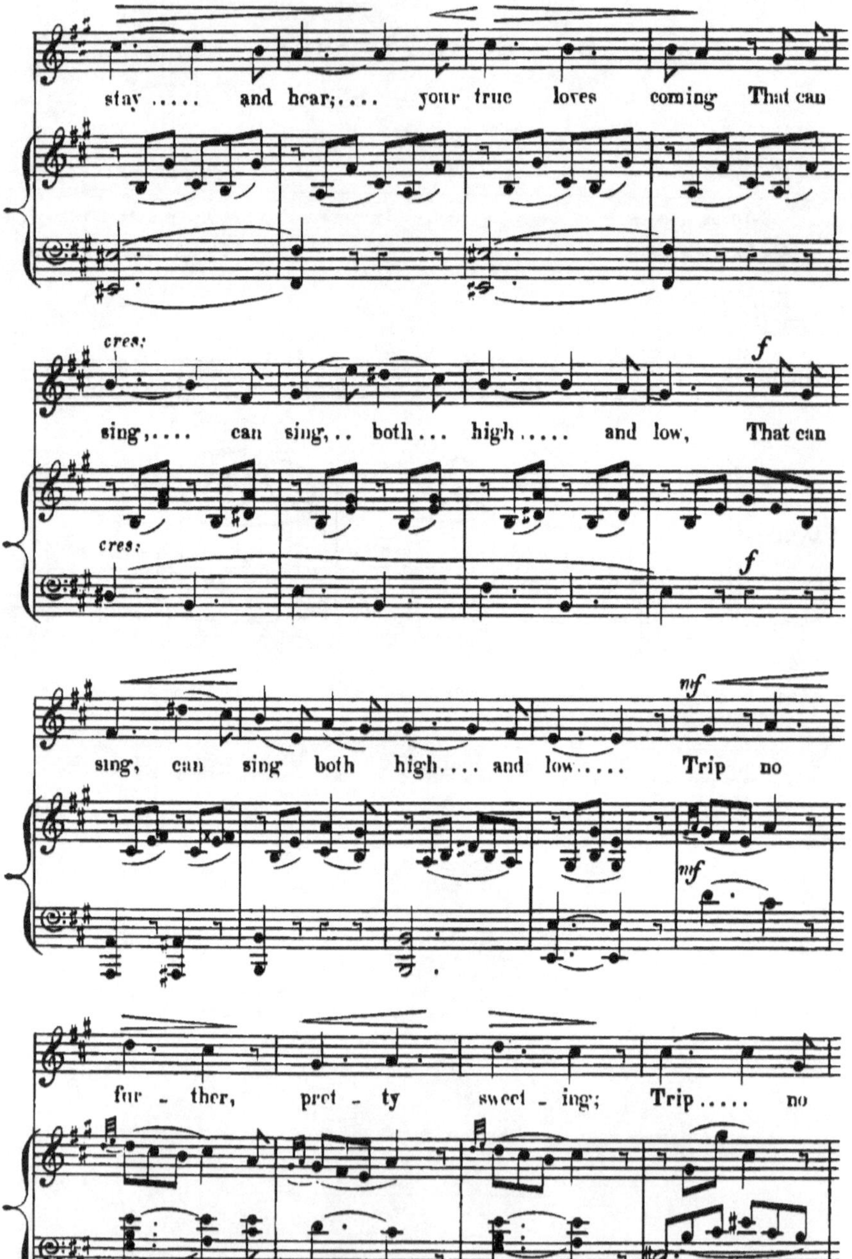
stay..... and hear;.... your true loves coming That can
cres:
f
sing,.... can sing,.. both... high..... and low, That can
cres:
f
mf
sing, can sing both high.... and low..... Trip no
mf
fur - ther, pret - ty sweet - ing; Trip..... no

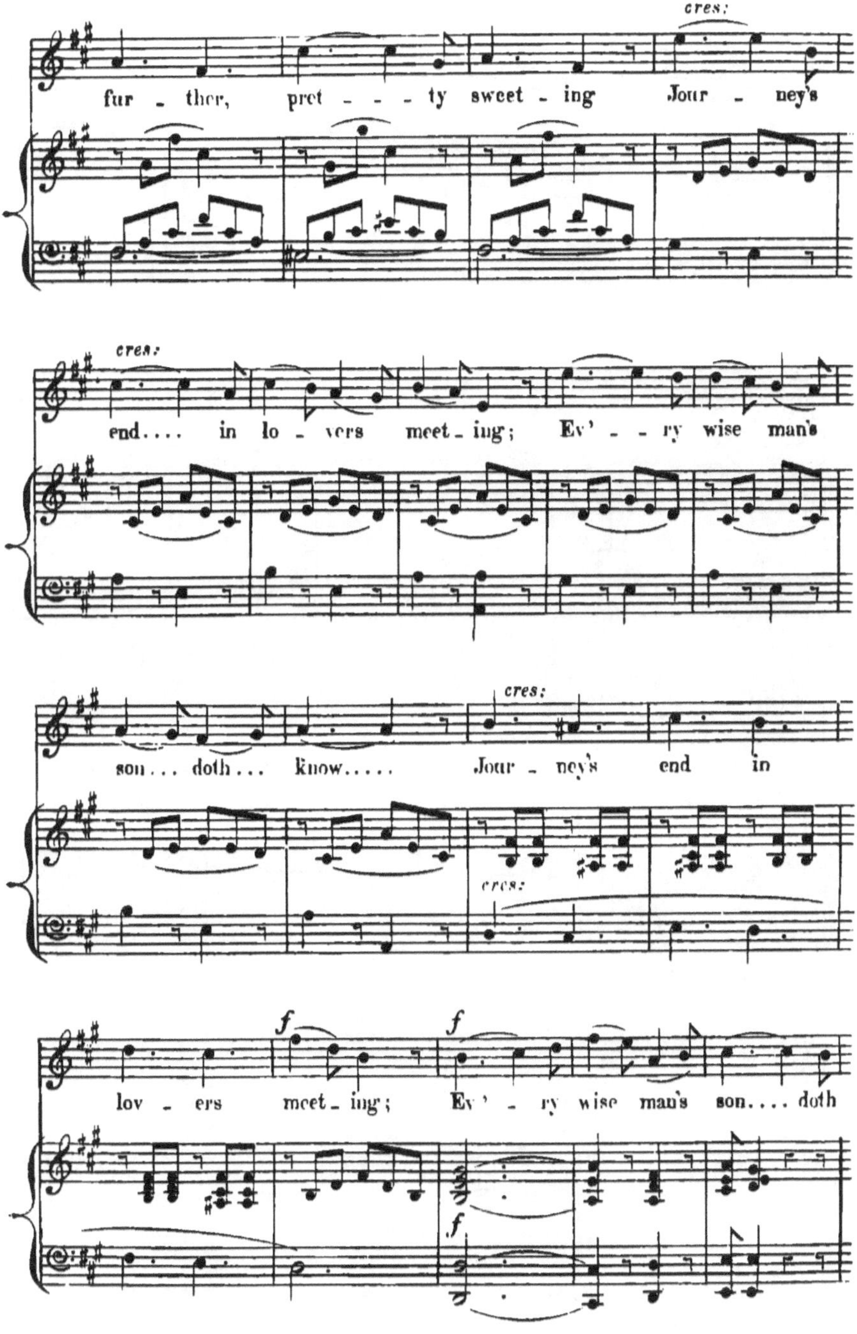
cres:
fur - ther, pret - - - ty sweet - ing Jour - ney's
cres:
end.... in lo - vers meet - ing; Ev' - - ry wise man's
cres:
son... doth... know..... Jour - ney's end in
cres:
f
f
lov - ers meet - ing; Ev' - ry wise man's son.... doth
f

JUNE, 1869.

HANOVER SQUARE,

A Magazine

OF

PIANOFORTE AND VOCAL MUSIC,

Edited by

LINDSAY SLOPER.

CASSELL, PETTER & GALPIN,
LA BELLE SAUVAGE YARD, LONDON, E.C.
AND 596, BROADWAY, NEW YORK.

"HANOVER SQUARE."
A Magazine of New Copyright Music,
EDITED BY LINDSAY SLOPER.

VOLS. I. II. AND III. NOW READY.

Price, elegantly bound in cloth, **SEVEN SHILLINGS AND SIXPENCE EACH.**

CONTENTS OF VOL. I.

No. 1.
Sorrows and Joys. Sketch for the Pianoforte ... Jules Benedict.
What does Little Birdie say? Song ... ... Arthur S. Sullivan.
Bright Hours. Caprice. Piano ... ... Sydney Smith.
Bessie Bell. Ballad ... ... Henry Smart.

No. 2.
Notturno. Pianoforte ... ... E. Silas.
Change upon Change. Song ... ... Virginia Gabriel.
   The Words by Elizabeth Barrett Browning.
The Gipsies' Revel. Piece for the Pianoforte ... Wilhelm Kuhe.
Though Age be like December. Song ... ... M. W. Balfe.
   The Words by Campbell Clarke.

No. 3.
Felice Notte. Barcarolle for the Pianoforte ... Ernst Pauer.
A Voice from the Sea. Song ... ... J. L. Hatton.
   The Words by W. S. Passmore.
Twelfth Night. Valse de Salon ... ... Brinley Richards.
The King's Daughter. Song ... ... Alex. Reichardt.
   The Words by Heinrich Heine. Translated by Wellington Guernsey

No. 4.
By the Lake. Reverie ... ... Lindsay Sloper.
Savourneen Deelish. Song ... ... Angelina.
   The Words by George Colman the younger.
Snowdrops. Pianoforte Piece ... ... Boyton Smith.
Forget Me Not. Song ... ... Wilhelm Ganz.
   The Words by Miss L. B. Courtenay.

No. 5.
Reveries-Valses. Piano ... ... Stephen Heller.
Kissing Her Hair. Song ... ... James L. Molloy.
   The Words by Algernon Charles Swinburne.
Galop de Concert. Piano ... ... Walter Macfarren.
River, Oh ! River. Song ... ... Elizabeth Philp.

No. 6.
Impromptu. Piano ... ... Lefébure Wely.
Echoes. Song ... ... Virginia Gabriel.
   The Words by Christina Rosetti.
Serenade. Piano ... ... Henry W. Goodban.
Stattene Allegro. Stornello ... ... Alberto Randegger.
   The English Translation by Campbell Clarke.

CONTENTS OF VOL. II.

No. 7.
Evening Rest. Berceuse. Piano ... ... Sydney Smith.
Love, the Pilgrim. Song ... ... Jacques Blumenthal.
   The Words by Hamilton Aidé.
Spring Breezes. Pianoforte Piece ... ... Ignace Gibsone.
It is the Golden May-time. Song ... ... J. L. Hatton.
   The Words by B. S. Montgomery.

No. 8.
A Lullaby. Pianoforte Piece ... ... Charles Salaman.
O fair Dove ! O fond Dove ! Song ... ... Arthur S. Sullivan.
   The Words by Miss Jean Ingelow.
La Vivandière. Marche brillante. Piano ... Edouard de Paris.
Sunshine after Cloud. Song ... ... Clara Gottschalk.
   The Words by W. Harrison.

No. 9.
A Moonlight Walk. Pianoforte ... ... G. A. Osborne.
Sleep, my Baby, Mother's near. A Slumber Song Albert Leaf.
Hunting Song. Impromptu for Piano ... ... { C. Swinnerton Heap
                                       (*MendelssohnScholar*).
Nobody's nigh to hear ... ... G. A. Macfarren.
   The Words by Miss Jean Ingelow.

No. 10.
Murmures. Nocturne-étude. Piano ... ... Charles A. Palmer.
It was a Lover and his Lass. Song ... ... F. Stanislaus.
   The Words by Shakespeare.
L'Etincelle. Morceau de Salon. Piano ... ... René Favarger.
Little Blossom. Ballad ... ... Virginia Gabriel.
   The Words by Alfred Thompson.

No. 11.
Flower-de-Luce. Reverie. Piano ... ... Walter Macfarren.
The Butterfly and the Flower. Song ... ... Alberto Randegger.
Le Sourire. Mazurka de Salon. Piano ... ... Henri Roubier.
Twenty Years Ago. Ballad ... ... E. L. Hime.
   The Words by J. E. Carpenter.

No. 12.
Shadow and Sunlight. Piano Piece ... ... W. Kuhe.
Ah, Love ! Ballad ... ... F. Hawtree.
   The Words by Longfellow.
Felice. Valse de Salon. Piano ... ... Lindsay Sloper.
Two Summer Days. Song ... ... Michael Watson.

CONTENTS OF VOL. III.

No. 13.
Happy Memories. Morceau de Salon. Piano... Sydney Smith.
A Farewell. Song ... ... Virginia Gabriel.
   The Words by Mrs. Frances Anne Kemble.
Bergeronnette, Styrienne. Piano ... ... M. Bergson.
Nora Creina. Song ... ... Alexander S Cooper.
   The Words by Thomas Moore.

No. 14.
Cantabile. Piano ... ... Charles Wehle.
Mary. Song ... ... G. A. Macfarren.
   The Words by Sir Walter Scott.
Rêve Espagnol. Serenade. Piano ... ... Edwin M. Lott.
'Twas long, long since, in the Spring time. Song G. B. Allen.
   The Words by Tom Hood.

No. 15.
Marche de Concert. Piano ... ... Walter Macfarren.
Wayward Thoughts. Song ... ... T. M. Mudie.
   The Words by Mrs. R. H. Foster.
Tears of Joy. Capriccietto ... ... Francesco Berger.
Ah ! Chloris. Pastoral ... ... Ignace Gibsone.
   The Words by Sir Charles Sedley.

No. 16.
Idylle. Piano ... ... C. Neustedt.
Oh ! to be a Sportive Fairy. Song ... ... J. L. Hatton.
   The Words by B. S. Montgomery.
The Song of the Brook. Pianoforte Piece ... E. A. Sydenham.
When Twilight Dews are falling soft. Song Evelyn Hampton.
   The Words by Thomas Moore.

No. 17.
Patrouille. Ronde de Nuit. Piano ... ... D. Magnus.
Spinning Song ... ... Virginia Gabriel.
   The Words by W. Storey.
Dancing Sea Spray. Morceau de Salon. Piano J. Theodore Trekell.
Autumn Song ... ... Henry Smart.
   The Words from the German.

No. 18.
Serenade. Piano ... ... Frederick H. Cowen.
Why, Lovely Charmer ? Song ... ... E. A. Sydenham.
   The Words by Sir Richard Steele.
L'Inconstante. Valse de Salon. Piano ... ... Polydore de Vos.
By the Sea. Ballad ... ... G. Richardson.
   The Words by C. O'Neill.

The separate Numbers are still to be had, Price **ONE SHILLING EACH.**

The **EXTRA CHRISTMAS NUMBER** consists entirely of New Dance Music. Price One Shilling.
Kellogg-Valse, Arditi,—Marie (Polka Mazurka), Gung'l—L'Ancien Regime (Quadrille on Old French Airs), Henry W. Goodban
Blush-Rose Waltz, Charles Godfrey,—Tintamarre Galop, Charles de Mazières.

LONDON: ASHDOWN AND PARRY, HANOVER SQUARE.

THE ELFIN HOME.

BY

W. KUHE.

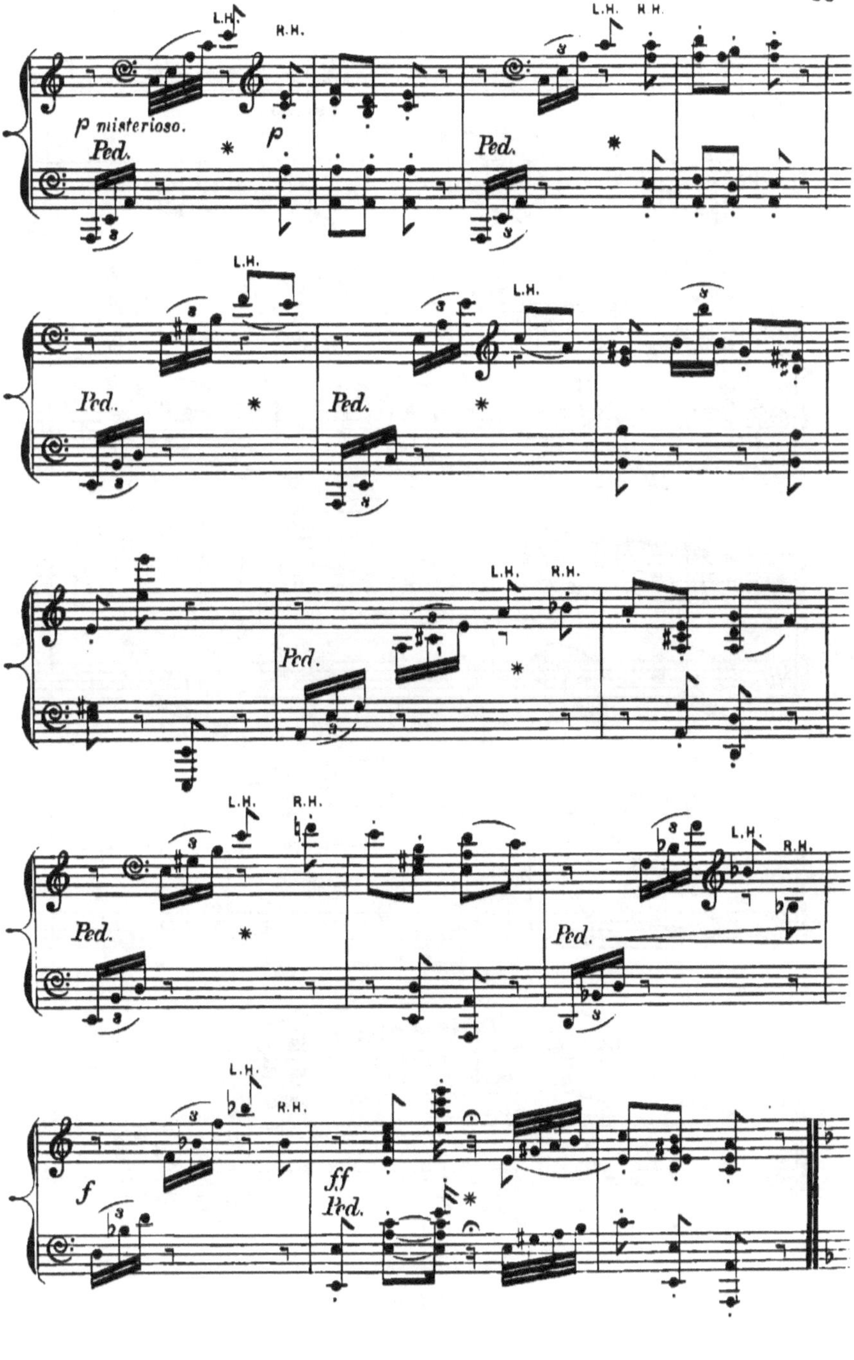
L.H.
R.H.
p misterioso.
Ped.
p
Ped.
Ped.
f
ff
Ped.

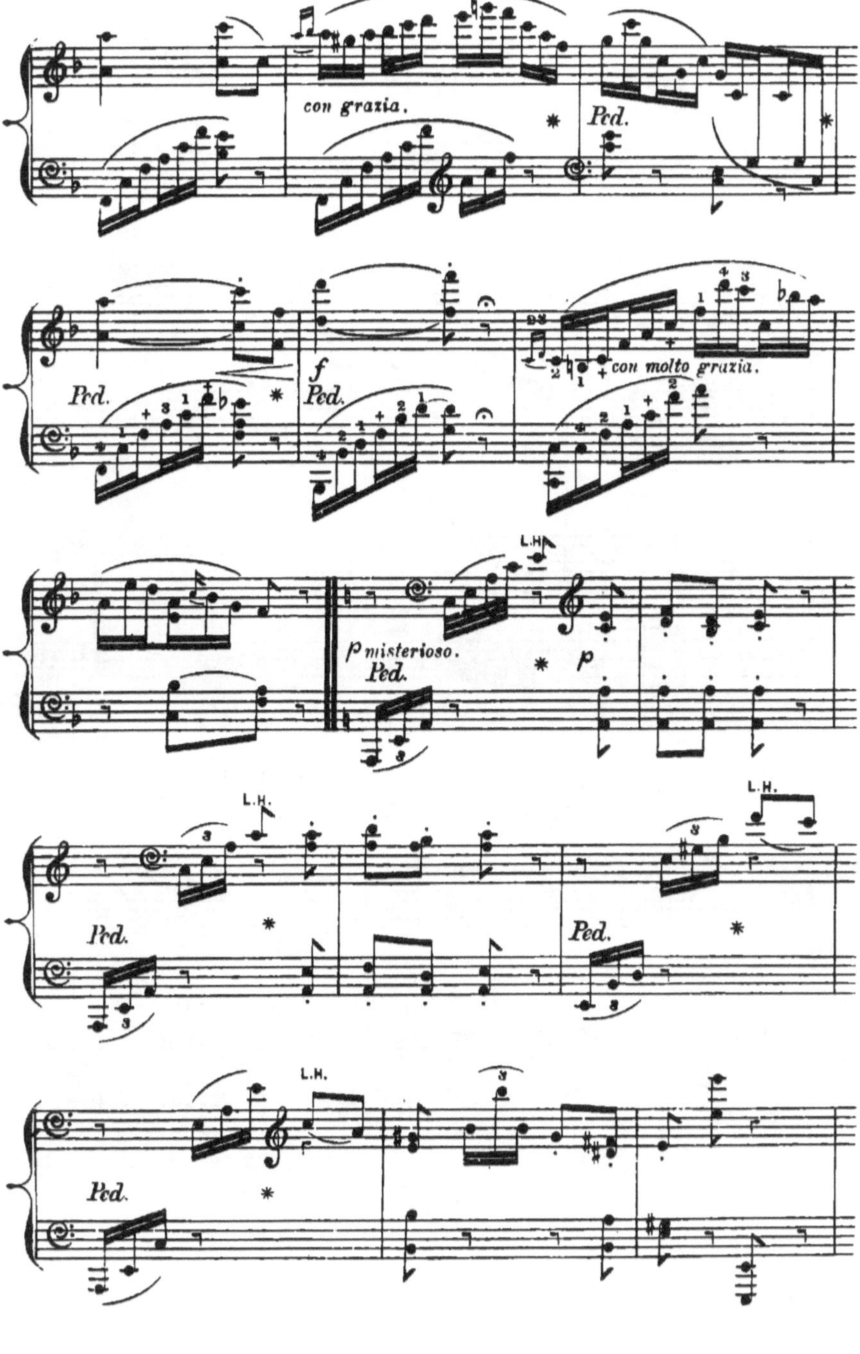
con grazia.
Ped.
Ped.
f
Ped.
con molto grazia.
p misterioso.
Ped.
p
L.H.
Ped.
L.H.
Ped.
L.H.
Ped.
L.H.

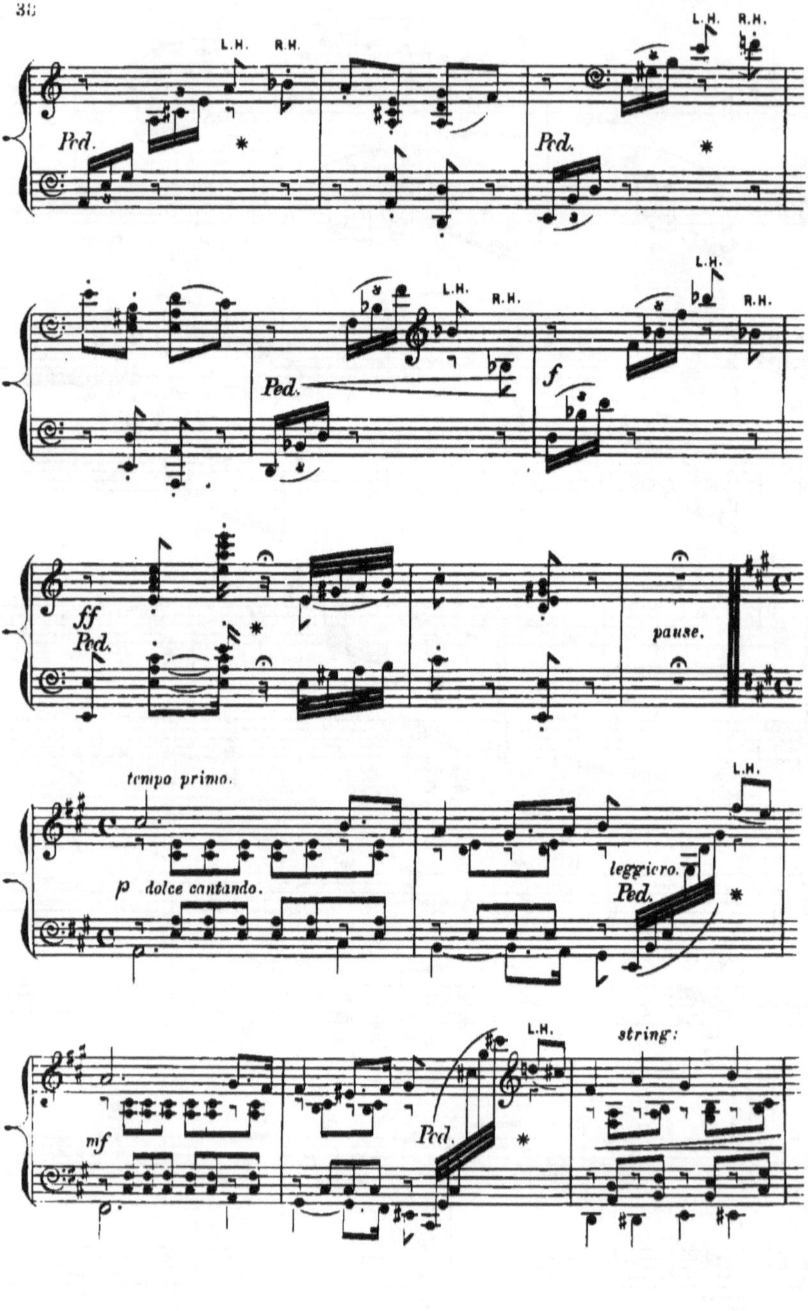
L.H.
R.H.
Ped.
f
ff
pause.
tempo primo.
p
dolce cantando.
leggiero.
mf
string:

AMY ROBSART.

SONG

Words by
HENRY FARNIE.

Music by
J. P. KNIGHT.

"The night wears on, and my Lord must soon arrive."
Kenilworth.

TO MISS COOTE.

CARINA.

ROMANCE

BY

WALTER MACFARREN.

50

HOPE FROM SORROW TAKES THE STING.

SONG

Composed by
W. MEYER LUTZ.

JULY, 1869

HANOVER SQUARE,

A Magazine

OF

PIANOFORTE AND VOCAL MUSIC,

Edited by

LINDSAY SLOPER.

CASSELL, PETTER & GALPIN,
LA BELLE SAUVAGE YARD, LONDON. E.C.
AND 596, BROADWAY, NEW YORK.

"HANOVER SQUARE,"
A Magazine of New Copyright Music,
EDITED BY LINDSAY SLOPER.

VOLS. I. II. AND III. NOW READY.
Price, elegantly bound in cloth, SEVEN SHILLINGS AND SIXPENCE EACH.

CONTENTS OF VOL. I.

No. 1.
Sorrows and Joys. Sketch for the Pianoforte ... Jules Benedict.
What does Little Birdie say? Song ... ... Arthur S. Sullivan.
Bright Hours. Caprice. Piano ... ... Sydney Smith.
Bessie Bell. Ballad ... ... Henry Smart.

No. 2.
Notturno. Pianoforte ... ... E. Silas.
Change upon Change. Song ... ... Virginia Gabriel.
 The Words by Elizabeth Barrett Browning.
The Gipsies' Revel. Piece for the Pianoforte ... Wilhelm Kuhe.
Though Age be like December. Song ... ... M. W. Balfe.
 The Words by Campbell Clarke.

No. 3.
Felice Notte. Barcarolle for the Pianoforte ... Ernst Pauer.
A Voice from the Sea. Song ... ... J. L. Hatton.
 The Words by W. S. Passmore.
Twelfth Night. Valse de Salon ... ... Brinley Richards.
The King's Daughter. Song ... ... Alex. Reichardt.
 The Words by Heinrich Heine. Translated by Wellington Guernsey.

No. 4.
By the Lake. Reverie ... ... Lindsay Sloper.
Savourneen Deelish. Song ... ... Angelina.
 The Words by George Colman the younger.
Snowdrops. Pianoforte Piece ... ... Boyton Smith.
Forget Me Not. Song ... ... Wilhelm Ganz.
 The Words by Miss L. B. Courtenay.

No. 5.
Reveries-Valses. Piano ... ... Stephen Heller.
Kissing Her Hair. Song ... ... James L. Molloy.
 The Words by Algernon Charles Swinburne.
Galop de Concert. Piano ... ... Walter Macfarren.
River, Oh! River. Song ... ... Elizabeth Philp.

No. 6.
Impromptu. Piano ... ... Leifbure Wely.
Echoes. Song ... ... Virginia Gabriel.
 The Words by Christina Rosetti.
Serenade. Piano ... ... Henry W. Goodban.
Stattene Allegro. Stornello ... ... Alberto Randegger.
 The English Translation by Campbell Clarke.

CONTENTS OF VOL. II.

No. 7.
Evening Rest. Berceuse. Piano ... ... Sydney Smith.
Love, the Pilgrim. Song ... ... Jacques Blumenthal.
 The Words by Hamilton Aidé.
Spring Breezes. Pianoforte Piece ... ... Ignace Gibsone.
It is the Golden May-time. Song ... ... J. L. Hatton.
 The Words by B. S. Montgomery.

No. 8.
A Lullaby. Pianoforte Piece ... ... Charles Salaman.
O fair Dove ! O fond Dove ! Song ... ... Arthur S. Sullivan.
 The Words by Miss Jean Ingelow.
La Vivandière. Marche brillante. Piano... ... Edouard de Paris.
Sunshine after Cloud. Song ... ... Clara Gottschalk.
 The Words by W. Harrison.

No. 9.
A Moonlight Walk. Pianoforte ... ... G. A. Osborne.
Sleep, my Baby, Mother's near. A Slumber Song Albert Laaf.
Hunting Song. Impromptu for Piano... ... C. Swinnerton Heap
 (*Mendelssohn Scholar*).
Nobody's nigh to hear ... ... G. A. Macfarren.
 The Words by Miss Jean Ingelow.

No. 10.
Murmures. Nocturne-étude. Piano ... ... Charles A. Palmer.
It was a Lover and his Lass. Song ... ... F. Stanislaus.
 The Words by Shakespeare.
L'Etincelle. Morceau de Salon. Piano ... ... René Favarger.
Little Blossom. Ballad ... ... Virginia Gabriel.
 The Words by Alfred Thompson.

No. 11.
Flower-de-Luce. Reverie. Piano ... ... Walter Macfarren.
The Butterfly and the Flower. Song ... ... Alberto Randegger.
Le Sourire. Mazurka de Salon. Piano ... ... Henri Roubier.
Twenty Years Ago. Ballad ... ... E. L. Hime.
 The Words by J. E. Carpenter.

No. 12.
Shadow and Sunlight. Piano Piece ... ... W. Kuhe.
Ah, Love! Ballad ... ... F. Hawtree.
 The Words by Longfellow.
Felice. Valse de Salon. Piano ... ... Lindsay Sloper.
Two Summer Days. Song ... ... Michael Watson.

CONTENTS OF VOL. III.

No. 13.
Happy Memories. Morceau de Salon. Piano... Sydney Smith.
A Farewell. Song ... ... Virginia Gabriel.
 The Words by Mrs. Frances Anne Kemble.
Bergeronnette, Styrienne. Piano ... ... M. Bergson.
Nora Creina. Song ... ... Alexander S. Cooper.
 The Words by Thomas Moore.

No. 14.
Cantabile. Piano ... ... Charles Wehle.
Mary. Song ... ... G. A. Macfarren.
 The Words by Sir Walter Scott.
Rêve Espagnol. Serenade. Piano ... ... Edwin M. Lott.
'Twas long, long since, in the Spring time. Song G. B. Allen.
 The Words by Tom Hood.

No. 15.
Marche de Concert. Piano ... ... Walter Macfarren.
Wayward Thoughts. Song ... ... T. M. Mudie.
 The Words by Mrs. R. H. Foster.
Tears of Joy. Capriccietto ... ... Francesco Berger.
Ah! Chloris. Pastoral ... ... Ignace Gibsone.
 The Words by Sir Charles Sedley.

No. 16.
Idylle. Piano ... ... C. Neustedt.
Oh ! to be a Sportive Fairy. Song ... ... J. L. Hatton.
 The Words by B. S. Montgomery.
The Song of the Brook. Pianoforte Piece... ... E. A. Sydenham.
When Twilight Dews are falling soft. Song ... Evelyn Hampton.
 The Words by Thomas Moore.

No. 17.
Patrouille. Ronde de Nuit. Piano ... ... D. Magnus.
Spinning Song ... ... Virginia Gabriel.
 The Words by W. Storey.
Dancing Sea Spray. Morceau de Salon. Piano J. Theodore Trekell.
Autumn Song ... ... Henry Smart.
 The Words from the German.

No. 18.
Serenade. Piano ... ... Frederick H. Cowen.
Why, Lovely Charmer? Song ... ... E. A. Sydenham.
 The Words by Sir Richard Steele.
L'Inconstante. Valse de Salon. Piano ... ... Polydore de Vos.
By the Sea. Ballad ... ... G. Richardson.
 The Words by C. O'Neill.

The separate Numbers are still to be had, Price ONE SHILLING EACH.

The **EXTRA CHRISTMAS NUMBER** consists entirely of New Dance Music. Price One Shilling.
Kellogg-Valse, Arditi.—Marie (Polka Mazurka), Gung'l—L'Ancien Regime (Quadrille on Old French Airs), Henry W. Goodban.
Blush-Rose Waltz, Charles Godfrey.—Tintamarre Galop, Charles de Mazières.

LONDON: ASHDOWN AND PARRY, HANOVER SQUARE.

LYDIA.

NOCTURNE

BY

IGNACE GIBSONE.

CARELESS AND FAITHFUL LOVE.

SONG

Words from
The "CYNOSURE."

Music by
FLORENCE A. MARSHALL.

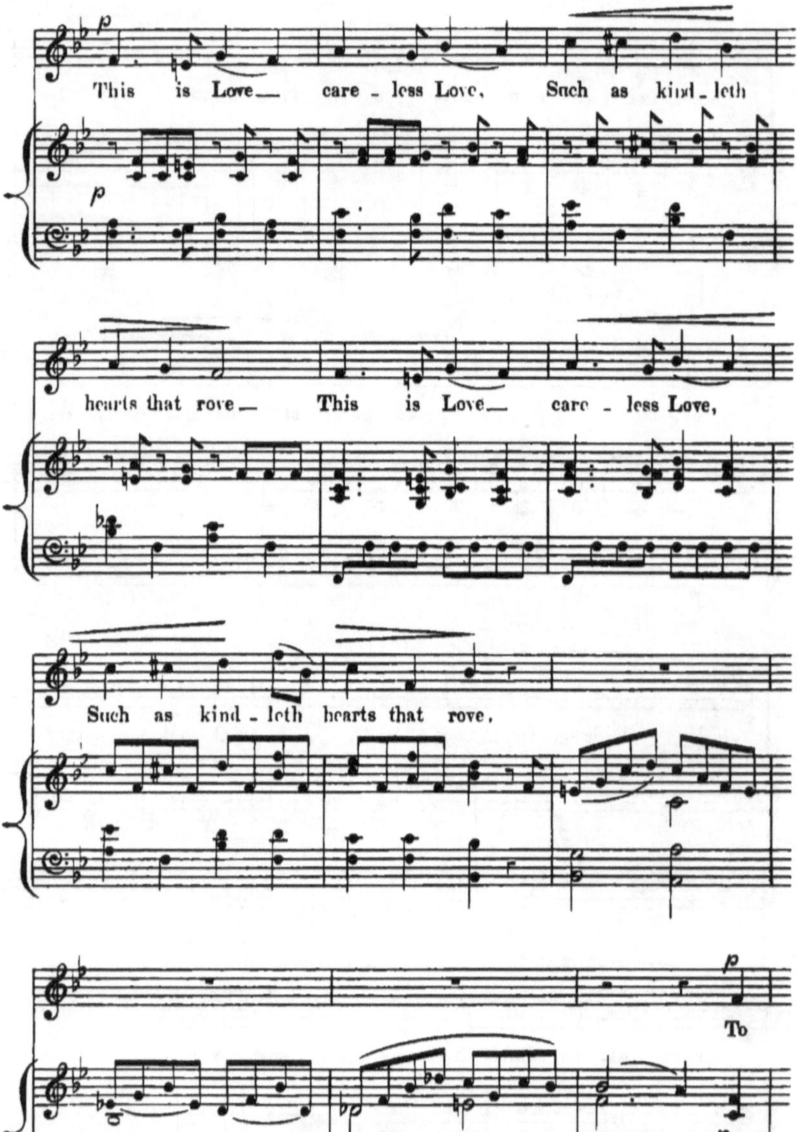
p
This is Love — care - less Love, Such as kind - leth
p
hearts that rove — This is Love — care - less Love,
Such as kind - leth hearts that rove,
p
To
p

VALSETTE.

BY

HAROLD THOMAS.

Mouvement de Valse.

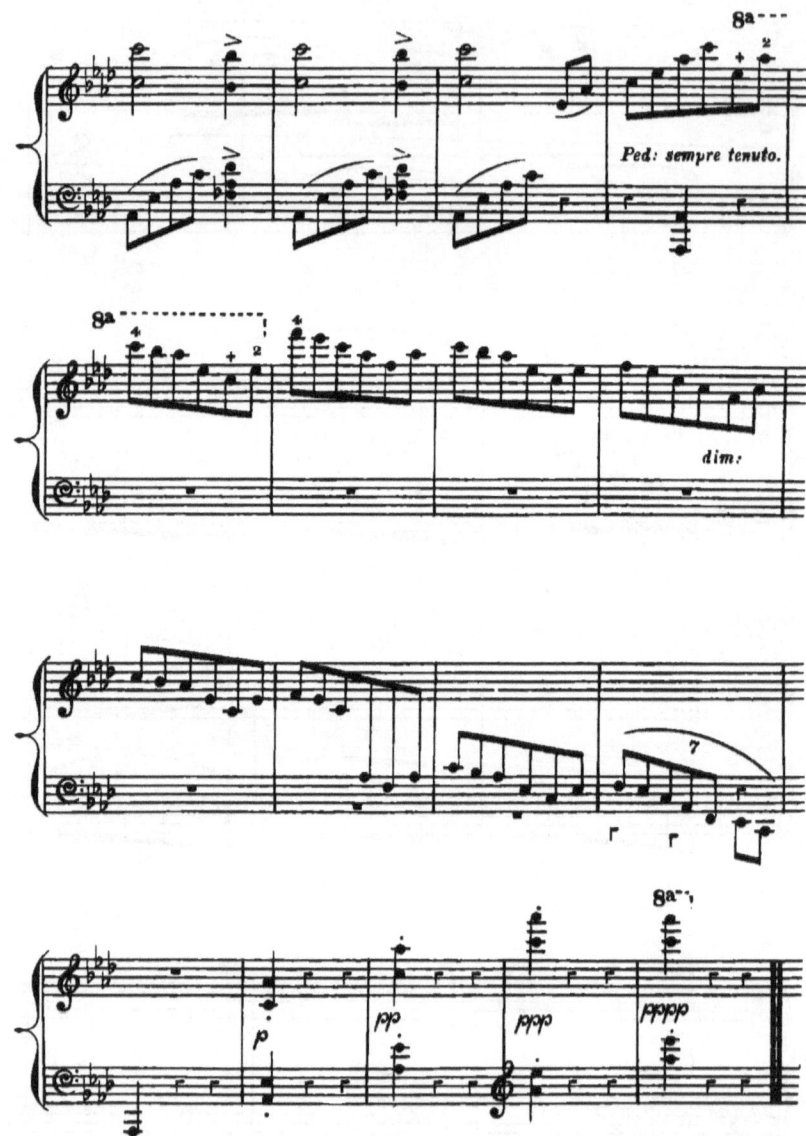

YOU'VE FORGOT THE COTTAGE DOOR

(LOVE'S REPROACH.)

BALLAD

Words by
CHARLES SWAIN.

Music by
FRANK MORI.

86

stream..... Where we two so oft_en met........ Watching

night's de_scend__ing beam.... O___ver

ritard: *tempo.*

clouds of ros_es set, Ah! You've for_got the cot_tage

door,   Where the sil__ver haw_thorn

AUGUST, 1869.

HANOVER SQUARE,

A Magazine

OF

PIANOFORTE AND VOCAL MUSIC,

Edited by

LINDSAY SLOPER.

CASSELL, PETTER & GALPIN,
LA BELLE SAUVAGE YARD, LONDON, E.C.
AND 596, BROADWAY, NEW YORK.

"HANOVER SQUARE,"
A Magazine of New Copyright Music,
EDITED BY LINDSAY SLOPER.

VOLS. I. II. AND III. NOW READY,
Price, elegantly bound in cloth, SEVEN SHILLINGS AND SIXPENCE EACH.

CONTENTS OF VOL. I.

No. 1.
Sorrows and Joys. Sketch for the Pianoforte ... Jules Benedict.
What does Little Birdie say? Song ... ... Arthur S. Sullivan.
Bright Hours. Caprice. Piano ... ... Sydney Smith.
Ossic Bell. Ballad ... ... Henry Smart.

No. 2.
Notturno. Pianoforte ... ... E. Silas.
Change upon Change. Song ... ... Virginia Gabriel.
The Words by Elizabeth Barrett Browning.
The Gipsies' Revel. Piece for the Pianoforte ... Wilhelm Kuhe.
Though Age be like December. Song ... ... M. W. Balfe.
The Words by Campbell Clarke.

No. 3.
Alice Notte. Barcarolle for the Pianoforte ... Ernst Pauer.
Voice from the Sea. Song ... ... J. L. Hatton.
The Words by W. S. Passmore.
Twelfth Night. Valse de Salon ... ... Brinley Richards.
The King's Daughter. Song ... ... Alex. Reichardt.
The Words by Heinrich Heine. Translated by Wellington Guernsey.

No. 4.
By the Lake. Reverie ... ... Lindsay Sloper.
Savourneen Deelish. Song ... ... Angelina.
The Words by George Colman the younger.
Snowdrops. Pianoforte Piece ... ... Boyton Smith.
Forget Me Not. Song ... ... Wilhelm Ganz.
The Words by Miss L. B. Courtenay.

No. 5.
Reveries-Valses. Piano ... ... Stephen Heller.
Kissing Her Hair. Song ... ... James L. Molloy.
The Words by Algernon Charles Swinburne.
Galop de Concert. Piano ... ... Walter Macfarren.
River, Oh! River. Song ... ... Elizabeth Philp.

No. 6.
Impromptu. Piano ... ... Lefébure Wely.
Echoes. Song ... ... Virginia Gabriel.
The Words by Christina Rosetti.
Serenade. Piano ... ... Henry W. Goodban.
Stattene Allegro. Stornello ... ... Alberto Randegger.
The English Translation by Campbell Clarke.

CONTENTS OF VOL. II.

No. 7.
Evening Rest. Berceuse. Piano ... ... Sydney Smith.
Love, the Pilgrim. Song ... ... Jacques Blumenthal.
The Words by Hamilton Aidé.
Spring Breezes. Pianoforte Piece ... ... Ignace Gibsone.
Is the Golden May-time. Song ... ... J. L. Hatton
The Words by B. S. Montgomery.

No. 8.
Lullaby. Pianoforte Piece ... ... Charles Salaman.
Fair Dove! O fond Dove! Song ... ... Arthur S. Sullivan.
The Words by Miss Jean Ingelow.
A Vivandière. Marche brillante. Piano ... Edouard de Paris.
Sunshine after Cloud. Song ... ... Clara Gottschalk.
The Words by W. Harrison.

No. 9.
Moonlight Walk. Pianoforte ... ... G. A. Osborne.
Sleep, my Baby, Mother's near. A Slumber Song Albert Leaf.
C. Swinnerton Heap
Hunting Song. Impromptu for Piano ... ... (Mendelssohn Scholar).
Nobody's nigh to hear ... ... G. A. Macfarren.
The Words by Miss Jean Ingelow.

No. 10.
Murmures. Nocturne-étude. Piano ... ... Charles A. Palmer.
It was a Lover and his Lass. Song ... ... F. Stanislaus.
The Words by Shakespeare.
L'Etincelle.' Morceau de Salon. Piano ... René Favarger.
Little Blossom. Ballad ... ... Virginia Gabriel.
The Words by Alfred Thompson.

No. 11.
Flower-de-Luce. Reverie. Piano ... ... Walter Macfarren.
The Butterfly and the Flower. Song ... ... Alberto Randegger.
Le Sourire. Mazurka de Salon. Piano ... Henri Roubier.
Twenty Years Ago. Ballad ... ... E. L. Hime.
The Words by J. E. Carpenter.

No. 12.
Shadow and Sunlight. Piano Piece ... ... W. Kuhe.
Ah, Love! Ballad ... ... F. Hawtree.
The Words by Longfellow.
Felice. Valse de Salon. Piano ... ... Lindsay Sloper.
Two Summer Days. Song ... ... Michael Watson.

CONTENTS OF VOL. III.

No. 13.
Happy Memories. Morceau de Salon. Piano... Sydney Smith.
Farewell. Song ... ... Virginia Gabriel.
The Words by Mrs. Frances Anne Kemble.
Bergeronnette, Styrienne. Piano ... ... M. Bergson.
Flora Crelus. Song ... ... Alexander S. Cooper.
The Words by Thomas Moore.

No. 14.
Cantabile. Piano ... ... Charles Wehle
Daisy. Song ... ... G. A. Macfarren.
The Words by Sir Walter Scott.
Ave Espagnol. Serenade. Piano ... ... Edwin M. Lott.
'Twas long, long since, in the Spring time. Song G. B. Allen.
The Words by Tom Hood.

No. 15.
Marche de Concert. Piano ... ... Walter Macfarren.
Wayward Thoughts. Song ... ... T. M. Mudie.
The Words by Mrs. R. H. Foster.
Tears of Joy. Capriccietto ... ... Francesco Berger.
Ah! Chloris. Pastoral ... ... Ignace Gibsone.
The Words by Sir Charles Sedley.

No. 16.
Idylle. Piano ... ... C. Neustedt.
Oh! to be a Sportive Fairy. Song ... ... J. L. Hatton.
The Words by B. S. Montgomery.
The Song of the Brook. Pianoforte Piece... E. A. Sydenham.
When Twilight Dews are falling soft. Song Evelyn Hampton.
The Words by Thomas Moore.

No. 17.
Patrouille. Ronde de Nuit. Piano ... ... D. Magnus.
Spinning Song ... ... Virginia Gabriel.
The Words by W. Storey.
Dancing Sea Spray. Morceau de Salon. Piano J. Theodore Trekell.
Autumn Song ... ... Henry Smart.
The Words from the German.

No. 18.
Serenade. Piano ... ... Frederick M. Cowen.
Why, Lovely Charmer? Song ... ... E. A. Sydenham.
The Words by Sir Richard Steele.
L'Inconstante. Valse de Salon. Piano ... Polydore de Vos.
By the Sea. Ballad ... ... G. Richardson.
The Words by C. O'Neill.

The separate Numbers are still to be had, Price ONE SHILLING EACH.

The **EXTRA CHRISTMAS NUMBER** consists entirely of New Dance Music. Price One Shilling.
Kellogg Valse, Arditi.—Marie (Polka Mazurka), Gung'l.—L'Ancien Regime (Quadrille on Old French Airs), Henry W. Goodban
Blush-Rose Waltz, Charles Godfrey.—Tintamarre Galop, Charles de Maziéres.

LONDON: ASHDOWN AND PARRY, HANOVER SQUARE.

LUSINGA.

BY

IMMANUEL LIEBICH.

DORA.

SONG

Words by
H. T. CRAVEN.

Music by
F. STANISLAUS.

TARANTELLE

BY

HENRY LAHEE.

III

DEDICATED TO MISS ALICE MAY.

IT SEEMS AS IF BUT YESTERDAY.

BALLAD

WORDS BY
J. ROSCOE.

MUSIC BY
G. B. ALLEN.

SEPTEMBER, 1869.

HANOVER SQUARE,

A Magazine

OF

PIANOFORTE AND VOCAL MUSIC,

Edited by

LINDSAY SLOPER.

CASSELL, PETTER & GALPIN,
LA BELLE SAUVAGE YARD, LONDON, E.C.
AND 596, BROADWAY, NEW YORK.

"HANOVER SQUARE."
A Magazine of New Copyright Music,
EDITED BY LINDSAY SLOPER.

VOLS. I. II. AND III. NOW READY.
Price, elegantly bound in cloth, SEVEN SHILLINGS AND SIXPENCE EACH.

CONTENTS OF VOL. I.

No. 1.
Sorrows and Joys. Sketch for the Pianoforte ... Jules Benedict.
What does Little Birdie say? Song ... Arthur S. Sullivan.
Bright Hours. Caprice. Piano ... Sydney Smith.
Bessie Bell. Ballad ... Henry Smart.

No. 2.
Notturno. Pianoforte ... E. Silas.
Change upon Change. Song ... Virginia Gabriel.
The Words by Elizabeth Barrett Browning.
The Gipsies' Revel. Piece for the Pianoforte ... Wilhelm Kuhe.
Though Age be like December. Song ... M. W. Balfe.
The Words by Campbell Clarke.

No. 3.
Felice Notte. Barcarolle for the Pianoforte ... Ernst Pauer.
A Voice from the Sea. Song ... J. L. Hatton.
The Words by W. S. Passmore.
Twelfth Night. Valse de Salon ... Brinley Richards.
The King's Daughter. Song ... Alex. Reichardt.
The Words by Heinrich Heine. Translated by Wellington Guernsey.

No. 4.
By the Lake. Reverie ... Lindsay Sloper.
Savourneen Deelish. Song ... Angelina.
The Words by George Colman the younger.
Snowdrops. Pianoforte Piece ... Boyton Smith.
Forget Me Not. Song ... Wilhelm Ganz.
The Words by Miss L. B. Courtenay.

No. 5.
Reveries-Valses. Piano ... Stephen Heller.
Kissing Her Hair. Song ... James L. Molloy.
The Words by Algernon Charles Swinburne.
Galop de Concert. Piano ... Walter Macfarren.
River, Oh! River. Song ... Elizabeth Philp.

No. 6.
Impromptu. Piano ... Lefébure Wely.
Echoes. Song ... Virginia Gabriel.
The Words by Christina Rosetti.
Serenade. Piano ... Henry W. Goodban.
Stattene Allegro. Stornello ... Alberto Randegger.
The English Translation by Campbell Clarke.

CONTENTS OF VOL. II.

No. 7.
Evening Rest. Berceuse. Piano ... Sydney Smith.
Love, the Pilgrim. Song ... Jacques Blumenthal.
The Words by Hamilton Aidé.
Spring Breezes. Pianoforte Piece ... Ignace Gibsone.
It is the Golden May-time. Song ... J. L. Hatton.
The Words by B. S. Montgomery.

No. 8.
A Lullaby. Pianoforte Piece ... Charles Salaman.
O fair Dove! O fond Dove! Song ... Arthur S. Sullivan.
The Words by Miss Jean Ingelow.
La Vivandière. Marche brillante. Piano ... Edouard de Paris.
Sunshine after Cloud. Song ... Clara Gottschalk.
The Words by W. Harrison.

No. 9.
A Moonlight Walk. Pianoforte ... G. A. Osborne.
Sleep, my Baby, Mother's near. A Slumber Song Albert Leaf.
Hunting Song. Impromptu for Piano ... C. Swinnerton Heap (*Mendelssohn Scholar*).
Nobody's nigh to hear ... G. A. Macfarren.
The Words by Miss Jean Ingelow.

No. 10.
Murmures. Nocturne-étude. Piano ... Charles A. Palmer.
It was a Lover and his Lass. Song ... F. Stanislaus.
The Words by Shakespeare.
L'Étincelle. Morceau de Salon. Piano ... René Favarger.
Little Blossom. Ballad ... Virginia Gabriel.
The Words by Alfred Thompson.

No. 11.
Flower-de-Luce. Reverie. Piano ... Walter Macfarren.
The Butterfly and the Flower. Song ... Alberto Randegger.
Le Sourire. Mazurka de Salon. Piano ... Henri Roubier.
Twenty Years Ago. Ballad ... E. L. Hime.
The Words by J. E. Carpenter.

No. 12.
Shadow and Sunlight. Piano Piece ... W. Kuhe.
Ah, Love! Ballad ... F. Hawtree.
The Words by Longfellow.
Felice. Valse de Salon. Piano ... Lindsay Sloper.
Two Summer Days. Song ... Michael Watson.

CONTENTS OF VOL. III.

No. 13.
Happy Memories. Morceau de Salon. Piano ... Sydney Smith.
A Farewell. Song ... Virginia Gabriel.
The Words by Mrs. Frances Anne Kemble.
Bergeronnette, Styrienne. Piano ... M. Bergson.
Nora Creina Song ... Alexander S. Cooper.
The Words by Thomas Moore.

No. 14.
Cantabile. Piano ... Charles Wehle.
Mary. Song ... G. A. Macfarren.
The Words by Sir Walter Scott.
Rêve Espagnol. Serenade. Piano ... Edwin M. Lott.
'Twas long, long since, in the Springtime. Song G. B. Allen.
The Words by Tom Hood.

No. 15.
Marche de Concert. Piano ... Walter Macfarren.
Wayward Thoughts. Song ... T. M. Mudie.
The Words by Mrs. R. H. Foster.
Tears of Joy. Capriccietto ... Francesco Berger.
Ah! Chloris. Pastoral ... Ignace Gibsone.
The Words by Sir Charles Sedley.

No. 16.
Idylle. Piano ... C. Neustedt.
Oh! to be a Sportive Fairy. Song ... J. L. Hatton.
The Words by B. S. Montgomery.
The Song of the Rose. Pianoforte Piece ... E. A. Sydenham.
When Twilight Dews are falling soft. Song ... Evelyn Hampton.
The Words by Thomas Moore.

No. 17.
Patrouille. Ronde de Nuit. Piano ... D. Magnus.
Spinning Song ... Virginia Gabriel.
The Words by W. Storey.
Dancing Sea Spray. Morceau de Salon. Piano J. Theodore Trevell.
Autumn Song ... Henry Smart.
The Words from the German.

No. 18.
Serenade. Piano ... Frederick H. Cowen.
Why, Lovely Charmer? Song ... E. A. Sydenham.
The Words by Sir Richard Steele.
L'Inconstante. Valse de Salon. Piano ... Polydore de Vos.
By the Sea. Ballad ... G. Richardson.
The Words by C. O'Neill.

The separate Numbers are still to be had, Price ONE SHILLING EACH.

The EXTRA CHRISTMAS NUMBER consists entirely of New Dance Music. Price One Shilling.
Kellogg-Valse, Arditi.—Marie (Polka Mazurka), Gung'l.—L'Ancien Regime (Quadrille on Old French Airs), Henry W. Goodban.
Blush-Rose Waltz, Charles Godfrey.—Tintamarre Galop, Charles de Maziéres.

LONDON: ASHDOWN AND PARRY, HANOVER SQUARE.

LE CHANT DES ALPES

IDYLLE

PAR

MICHEL BERGSON.

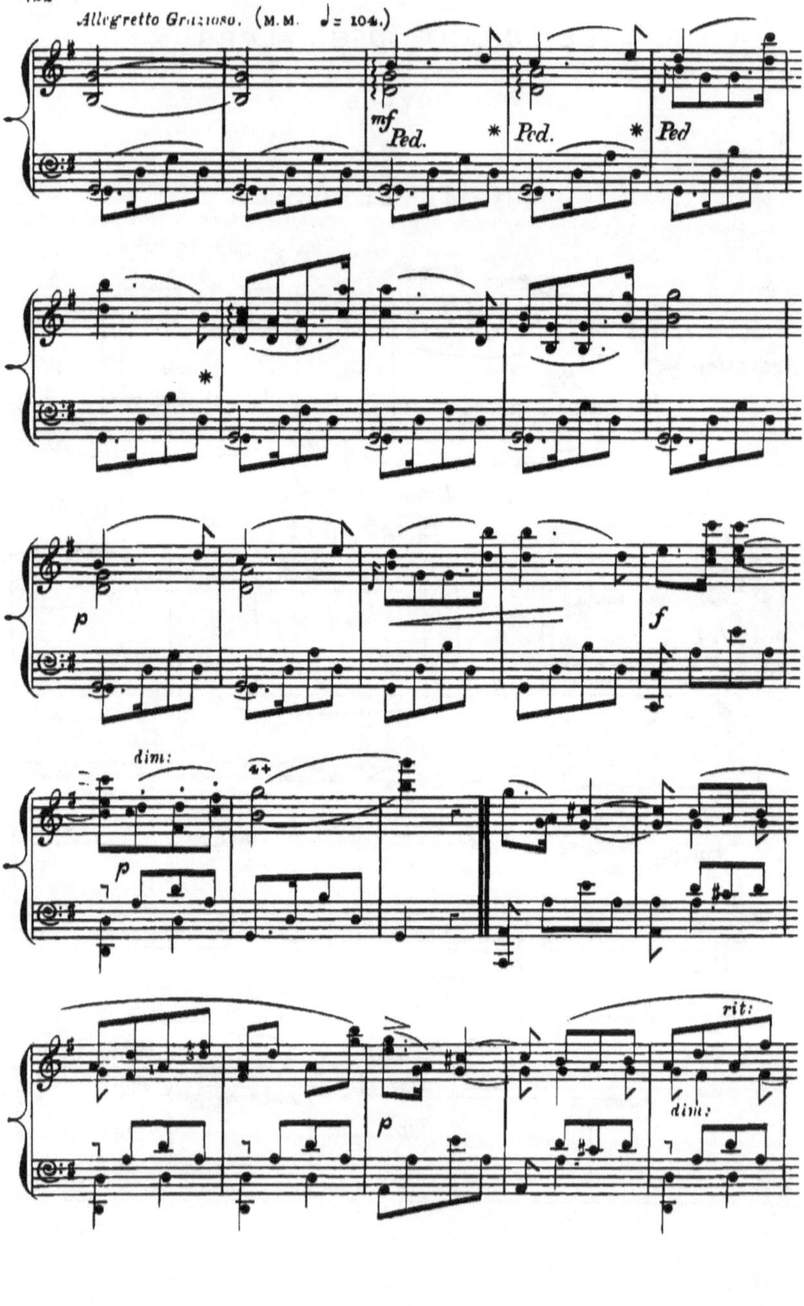
Allegretto Grazioso. (M.M. ♩= 104.)
mf
Ped.
*
Ped.
*
Ped
*
p
f
dim:
p
p
rit:
dim:

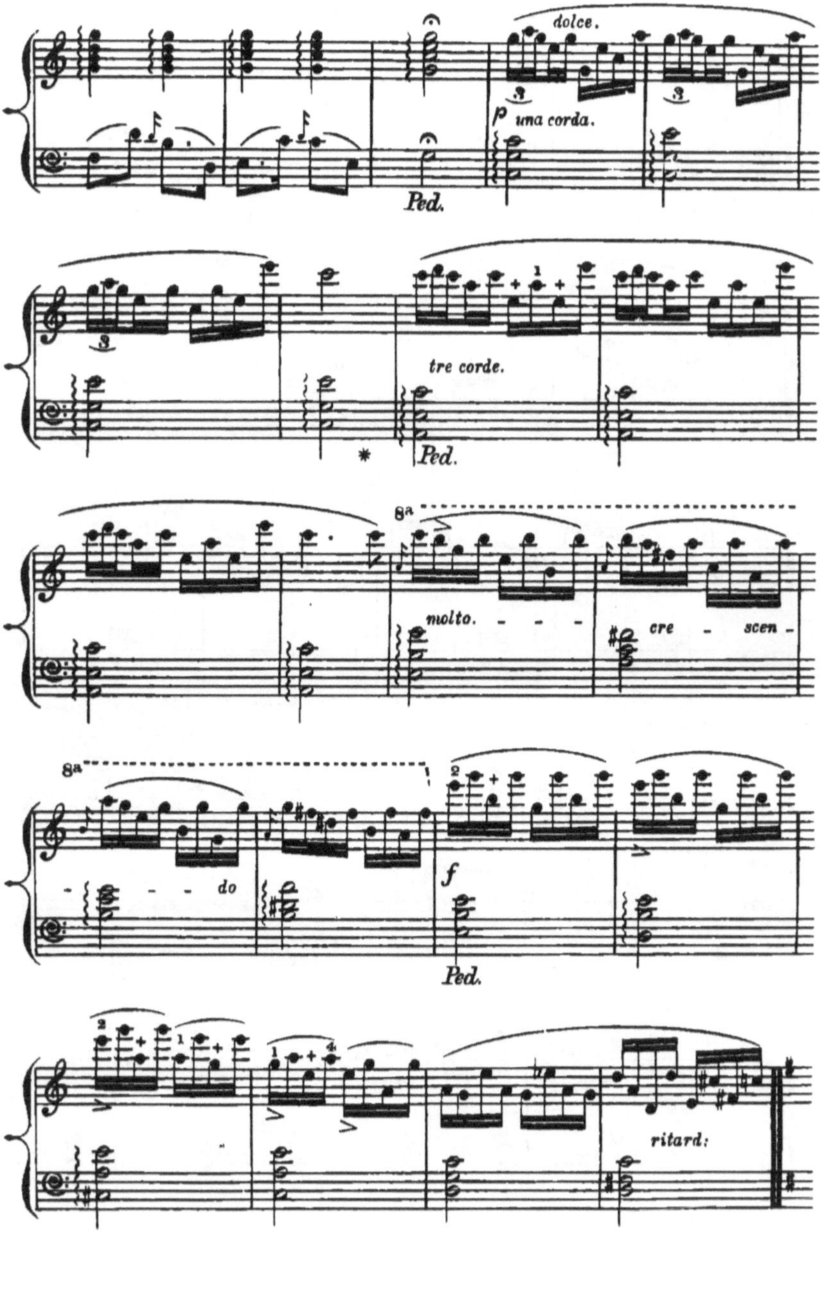
dolce.
p una corda.
Ped.
tre corde.
Ped.
8a
molto. - - -
cre - scen -
- - - do
f
Ped.
ritard:

DO THEY KNOW IT?

SONG.

Music by
LINDSAY SLOPER.

lark, from the corn up-spring-ing, Scatt-'ring

songs like drops of dew, Know how

sweet, on the soul of sor - row, Fall those wild

notes ten-der and true? Does he

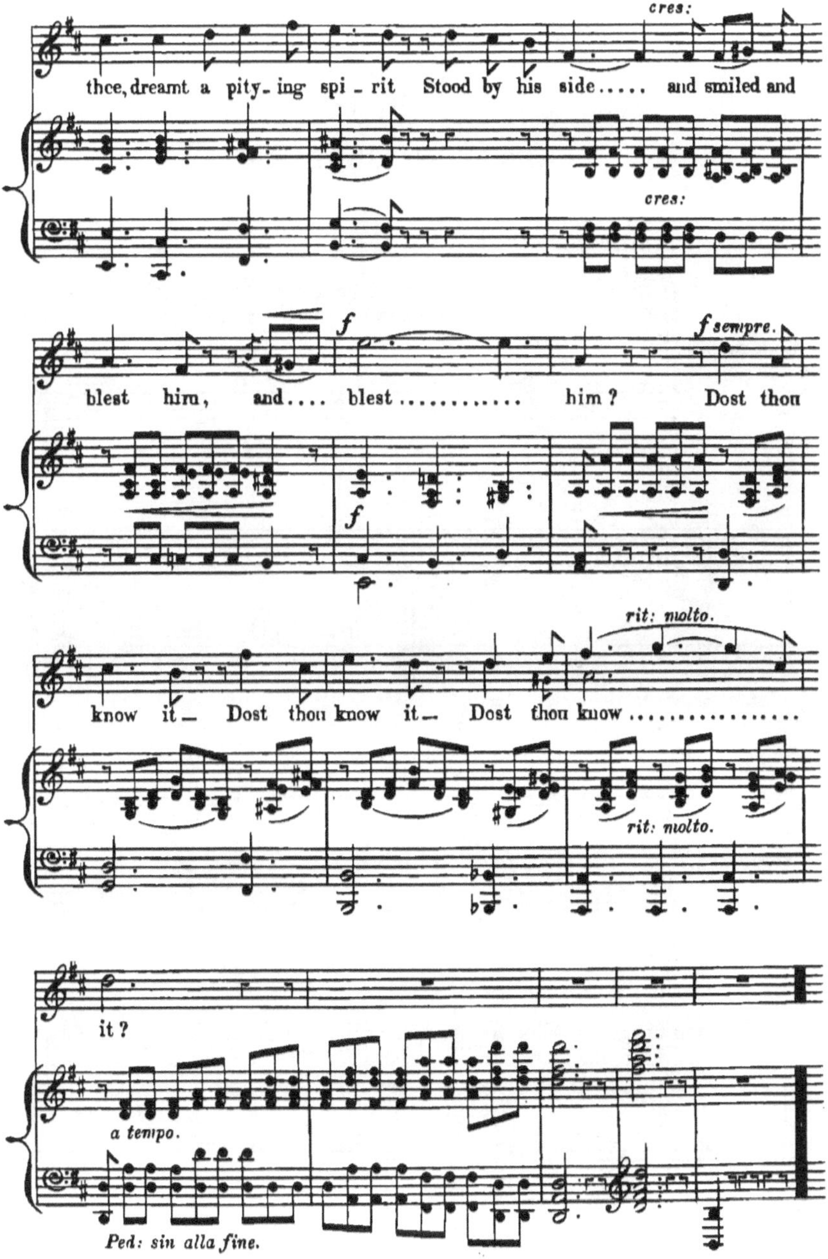
cres:
thee, dreamt a pity_ing spi_rit Stood by his side..... and smiled and
cres:
f
blest him, and.... blest............ him? Dost thou
f sempre.
f
rit: molto.
know it_ Dost thou know it_ Dost thou know................
rit: molto.
it?
a tempo.
Ped: sin alla fine.

SPRING LEAVES

BY

HENRY W. GOOBLAN.

LEILA'S DEPARTURE.

BALLAD

Music by
OLIVERIA PRESCOTT.

OCTOBER, 1869.

HANOVER SQUARE,

A Magazine

OF

PIANOFORTE AND VOCAL MUSIC,

Edited by

LINDSAY SLOPER.

CASSELL, PETTER & GALPIN,
LA BELLE SAUVAGE YARD, LONDON, E.C.
AND 596, BROADWAY, NEW YORK.

"HANOVER SQUARE,"
A Magazine of New Copyright Music,
EDITED BY LINDSAY SLOPER

VOLS. I. II. AND III. NOW READY.

Price elegantly bound in cloth, SEVEN SHILLINGS AND SIXPENCE EACH.

CONTENTS OF VOL. I.

No. 1.
- Sorrows and Joys. Sketch for the Pianoforte ... Jules Benedict.
- What does Little Birdie say? Song ... Amber S. Sullivan
- Bright Hours. Caprice, Piano ... Sydney Smith.
- Music Bell. Ballad ... Henry Smart

No. 2.
- Notturno. Pianoforte ... E. Silas.
- Change upon Change. Song ... Virginia Gabriel
  - The Words by Elizabeth Barrett Browning.
- The Gipsies' Revel. Piece for the Pianoforte ... Wilhelm Kuhe.
- Though Age be like December. Song ... M W Balfe
  - The Words by Campbell Clarke.

No. 3.
- Felice Notte. Barcarolle for the Pianoforte ... Ernst Pauer.
- A Voice from the Sea. Song ... J. L. Hatton.
  - The Words by W. S. Passmore.
- Twelfth Night. Valse de Salon ... Brinley Richards.
- The King's Daughter. Song ... Alex. Reichardt.
  - The Words by Heinrich Heine Translated by Wellington Guernsey.

No. 4.
- By the Lake. Reverie ... Lindsay Sloper.
- Savourneen Deelish. Song ... Angelina.
  - The Words by George Colman the younger.
- Snowdrops. Pianoforte Piece ... Boyton Smith.
- Forget Me Not. Song ... Wilhelm Ganz.
  - The Words by Miss L. B. Courtenay.

No. 5.
- Reveries-Valses. Piano ... Stephen Heller.
- Kissing Her Hair. Song ... James L. Molloy
  - The Words by Algernon Charles Swinburne.
- Galop de Concert. Piano ... Walter Macfarren.
- River, Oh! River. Song ... Elizabeth Philp.

No. 6.
- Impromptu. Piano ... Leffbure Wely.
- Echoes. Song ... Virginia Gabriel
  - The Words by Christina Rosetti.
- Serenade. Piano ... Henry W. Goodban.
- Stattene Allegro. Stornello ... Alberto Randegger
  - The English Translation by Campbell Clarke.

CONTENTS OF VOL. II.

No. 7.
- Evening Rest. Berceuse Piano ... Sydney Smith.
- Love the Pilgrim. Song ... Jacques Blumenthal.
  - The Words by Hamilton Aidé.
- Spring Breezes. Pianoforte Piece ... Ignace Gibsone
- Golden May-time. Song ... J. L. Hatton
  - The Words by B. S. Montgomery.

No. 8.
- A Lullaby. Pianoforte Piece ... Charles Salaman.
- O fair Dove! O fond Dove! Song ... Arthur S. Sullivan
  - The Words by Miss Jean Ingelow.
- La Vivandière. Marche brillante. Piano ... Edouard de Paris
- Sunshine after Cloud. Song ... Clara Gottschalk
  - The Words by W. Harrison.

No. 9.
- A Moonlight Walk. Pianoforte ... G. A. Osborne.
- Sleep, my Baby, Mother's near. A Slumber Song ... Albert Leaf.
- Hunting Song. Impromptu for Piano ... C. Swinnerton Heap
  ... (Mendelssohn Scholar).
- Nobody's nigh to hear ... G. A. Macfarren.
  - The Words by Miss Jean Ingelow.

No. 10.
- Murmures. Nocturne-étude Piano ... Charles A. Palmer.
- It was a Lover and his Lass. Song ... F. Stanislaus.
  - The Words by Shakespeare.
- L'Etincelle. Morceau de Salon. Piano ... René Favarger.
- Little Blossom. Ballad ... Virginia Gabriel.
  - The Words by Alfred Thompson

No. 11.
- Flower-de-Luce. Reverie. Piano ... Walter Macfarren.
- The Butterfly and the Flower. Song ... Alberto Randegger
- Le Sourire. Mazurka de Salon. Piano ... Henri Roubier.
- Twenty Years Ago. Ballad ... E. L. Hime.
  - The Words by J. E. Carpenter.

No. 12.
- Shadow and Sunlight. Piano Piece ... W. Kuhe.
- Ah, Love! Ballad ... F Hawtree
  - The Words by Longfellow.
- Felice. Valse de Salon. Piano ... Lindsay Sloper.
- Two Summer Days. Song ... Michael Watson.

CONTENTS OF VOL. III.

No. 13.
- Happy Memories. Morceau de Salon. Piano ... Sydney Smith.
- Farewell. Song ... Virginia Gabriel
  - The Words by Mrs. Frances Anne Kemble
- Margueritte. Styrienne. Piano ... M. Bergson.
- Sweet Croina. Song ... Alexander S Cooper.
  - The Words by Thomas Moore

No. 14.
- Cantabile. Piano ... Charles Wehle
- Mary. Song ... G. A. Macfarren.
  - The Words by Sir Walter Scott.
- Rêve Espagnol. Serenade. Piano ... Edwin M. Lott.
- I was long, long since, in the Spring time. Song ... G. B. Allen.
  - The Words by Tom Hood

No. 15.
- Marche de Concert. Piano ... Walter Macfarren.
- Wayward Thoughts. Song ... T. M. Mudie
  - The Words by Mrs. R. H. Foster.
- Tears of Joy. Capriccietto ... Francesco Berger
- Ah! Chloris. Pastoral ... Ignace Gibsone.
  - The Words by Sir Charles Sedley.

No. 16.
- Idylle. Piano ... C. Neustedt
- Oh! to be a Sportive Fairy. Song ... J. L. Hatton.
  - The Words by B. S. Montgomery.
- The Song of the Brook. Pianoforte Piece. E. A. Sydenham
- When Twilight Dews are falling soft. Song ... Evelyn Hampton.
  - The Words by Thomas Moore.

No. 17.
- Patrouille. Ronde de Nuit. Piano ... D. Magnus.
- Spinning Song ... Virginia Gabriel.
  - The Words by W Storey
- Dancing Sea Spray. Morceau. Salon. Piano J. Theodore Trekell.
- Autumn Song ... Henry Smart.
  - The Words from the German.

No. 18.
- Serenade. Piano ... Frederick H. Cowen.
- Why, Lovely Charmer? Song ... E A. Sydenham.
  - The Words by Sir Richard Steele.
- L'Inconstante. Valse de Salon. Piano ... Polydore de Vos
- By the Sea. Ballad ... G. Richardson.
  - The Words by C. O'Neill.

The separate Numbers are still to be had, Price ONE SHILLING EACH.

The EXTRA CHRISTMAS NUMBER consists entirely of New Dance Music. Price One Shilling.

Scherzo-Valse, Arditi.—Marie (Polka Mazurka), Gung'l.—L'Ancien Regime (Quadrille on Old French Airs), Henry W. G...—
Blush-Rose Waltz. Charles Godfrey.—Tintamarre Galop, Charles de Mazières.

LONDON, ASHDOWN & PARRY, HANOVER SQUARE

LA ZINGARA

CHARACTERISTIC PIECE
BY
LINDSAY SLOPER.

I LAID HIS HEAD.

BALLAD.

Words by
C. D. WYNDER.

Music by
W. H. GILL.

round his hair;..... The winds make mu - - - sic of his name,..... And mourn for one so fair, so fair...... Lul - - - la - by......

rall
Lul - - la - by.....
colla voce. *f a tempo.*

VALSE STYRIENNE

BY

CHARLES DE MAZIÈRES.

I CANNOT TELL THEE WHY I LOVE

BALLAD

Words by
J. N. COOPER.

Music by
JOHN H. L. GLO.

178

www.ingramcontent.com/pod-product-compliance
Lightning Source LLC
Chambersburg PA
CBHW032136160426
43197CB00008B/669